On Dufur Hill

For Melinda –
Enjoy Dufur!.

Penelope

Dufur

population: 623
location: Wasco County, north-central Oregon
chief product: wheat
annual rainfall:12 inches
origin of name: early settlers Andrew and Enoch Dufur
pronunciation of name: DOO-fur
town motto: *See what Dufur can do for you*

On Dufur Hill

Dear wind, why am I carrying this tumbleweed
down the hill? It would blow down on its own.

When tumbleweed tumbles down Main Street, Ron
at Ace Hardware, Charla at Kramer's Market, Dave
at the post office, Josiah at the Balch Hotel, each
one in turn, will stand at a well-used wooden
counter and watch it roll by.

Tumbleweed never stops to purchase anything. It
already has everything it needs.

Poems by Penelope Scambly Schott

Turning Point

Published by Turning Point
P.O. Box 541106
Cincinnati, OH 45254-1106

ISBN: 9781625493453

Poetry Editor: Kevin Walzer
Business Editor: Lori Jareo

Cover photo by Sam Beebe/Ecotrust

This image, which was originally posted to Panoramio, was automatically
reviewed on 21 June 2016 by Panoramio upload bot, who confirmed that it was
available on Panoramio under the above license on that date.

CC BY-SA 3.0
File:Dufur, Oregon - panoramio.jpg
Created: 18 June 2008
Location: 45° 27' 13.06" N, 121° 7' 40.96" W

Cover design by Eric Sweetman

Visit us on the web at www.turningpointbooks.com

Acknowledgments

Several of these poems have appeared in the following publications:

Artful Dodge
Calyx
Connecticut River Reiew
Gold Man
Gyroscope
Inflectionist Review
Panoply
Pebble Poetry
Postcard Poems
Potomac Review
Rat's Ass Review
Raven's Perch
Timberline Review
Williwaw
Windfall

One poem was a prizewinner in the Goldendale, Washington radio contest and another received first prize in an Oregon Poetry Association contest. A third is used as an example in *The Practicing Poet: Writing Beyond the Basics*, edited by Diane Lockward. Two appeared on the political website *New Verse News*.

To the memory of Everett Marvel, 1922-2017

August 18, 2017

– for E.M.

We buried him in high morning.
Afternoon spilled vivid sunlight

until the sun fell behind the hill.
Twilight. Full dark. I wanted

to go back to the cemetery.
Maybe, yes, I almost believed

he might feel someone there.
I could sleep on the new grave

just so he wouldn't be all alone
through this first night.

Table of Contents

HOME GALAXY

INVITATION

Driving to Dufur

So you take I-84 east out of Portland
where it follows the wide Columbia out through the Gorge
to a landscape of waterfalls and steep basalt cliffs,
past Cascade Locks where the river carved through the mountains,
and if it's raining anywhere, it's also raining here,
if the road is icy anywhere, it's certainly icy here,
and then you watch for the triangle of Wind Mountain,
and the high meadows of Dog Mountain,
and you picture those expanses of yellow balsamroot
broken only by orange paintbrush and lavender-blue columbine,
until you remember it's still winter and still raining
both here and back in Portland where it will go on raining
until the fifth of July,
so you keep driving east until the sky
shows patches of blue,
and by the time you have passed Hood River
the blue patches get larger
and the hills on one side of the river
have started drying out and then on both sides,
and when you pass that railroad tunnel right before Mosier
where you cross the line into Wasco County,
you are grinning
like a kid on the first morning of summer vacation,
and by the time you get to The Dalles
the sky is entirely blue,
and you catch yourself humming,
and at exit 87 you turn south onto route 197,
heading up Auction hill where the road becomes two lanes
briefly,
but just as you are starting to speed you remember
that one time you got stopped by the sheriff
and had to go to traffic school
where the instructor told you how to avoid the cops,
so you slow down

between cherry orchards and wheat fields
to exactly eight miles over the speed limit,
passing the sign that says
Leaving the National Scenic Area
where, immediately after the sign,
the hills get even more beautiful
as you pass Five Mile and Eight Mile
and the turn-off to Rice,
a town which no longer exists,
and you pass the turn-off to Boyd,
which barely exists,
until you see a square of trees ahead
which will be Dufur cemetery
where you own a plot between two sets of friends,
one couple buried and the other busily alive,
and your plot has a full view of Mount Hood
even though when you finally reside there
you'll be under the ground,
but you still like the view
so maybe you should put a bench there,
but today you don't stop,
and in less than a mile you veer slightly right
to come down into Dufur on Court Street,
remembering to slow to 25 mph
as you pass the field of retired combines
resting like ancient beasts
and the ranger station,
and then, if the new yellow caution sign is flashing
because school is in session, you slow down to 20,
until just before the school but after the Grace Church,
which looks like an old western storefront,
here's this little lavender house with a light green roof
and a white screen door with curlicues,
and the sign by the door reads WELCOME,
but you already know that you are so welcome,
more welcome
than you have ever felt in all your whole long life,

and you can forgive everyone who ever did you wrong
whether by ill-will or accident,
because you know that the chairs and the desk
and the bed with the high headboard and its garland
of raised and painted flowers,
the coffee pot and your books,
your grandmother's pedestal bowl,
the bathtub asleep on its four clawed feet,
and the white curtains tied back with ribbons
are all like you left them, just like you like them,
just like the house has been calling for you.

Here's the key warm in your hand.

Trying to Show You

Up here the horizon makes a circle
with bumps for the mountains.
From Dufur Hill I can see my house,
two states, and parts of seven counties.

These high wheat fields are golden
even if it's a cliché to say so.
I could use ochre or yellow madder
but really the wheat is intensely golden

and while I'm giving you color words
a red combine comes carving a pattern
through the high ripe wheat,
its red a red between brick and maroon.

Now the combine is headed right at me.
I want to snap a photo with my phone
but the sunlight is so damn brilliant
that I can't see which symbol to press.

That's why I have to write this down.
You, reader, aren't up here with me
so no use shouting *Look at this.*
I wish I could show it to my dead father

but what good in wishing? *Look,* I'd say,
how wheat dust rises to float and settle
over headless stubble. Here's my plan:
to share this town with everyone I love.

Calling the Meeting to Order

Here they all are, assembled around me:
Mount Adams to the north,
Mount Saint Helens with the blown-off top,
our local Mount Hood,
and, peeking up in the south, the pointy tips
of Mount Jefferson,
each peak bright with snow.

Hear ye, oh mighty mountains.
Why do I convene you thus?

Because our town needs you
for greening slopes of winter wheat,
for heifers and calves grazing in stubble,
for the snow that melts into Fifteen Mile Creek,
for knowing our way home.

Welcome, tall friends, to our meeting.
Let us proceed with the beautiful minutes.

Frequently Asked Questions after a Poetry Reading

Where do you find ideas for poems?
What time of the day do you write?

Poems are easier to find if you get up early.
Me, I hunt for poems on top of Dufur Hill.

I start by tying my sneakers with double knots
before the dog and I head out for our walk.

It's like a quarter of a mile to the cattle gate
where I'm always careful to re-latch the chain.

Then we climb. Often I bend down to sniff.
My wise dog has taught me so much.

A bush that looks like but isn't sagebrush
tastes vaguely of licorice or maybe lemon.

Some days poems pile up like tumbleweed
but other times I have to wait a little longer.

The real trick is to sneak up on a poem.
I sit on my same rock counting mountains

as if I didn't care about words. After awhile
the dog lies down in the shade of my knees

and I look west toward the forest or east
toward the plains or beyond the Columbia

or south for the small tip of Mount Jefferson
where it pokes over the line of Tygh ridge,

until the world is in place. And then, bingo!
I hear my voice speaking a poem out loud.

The rest is easy. I keep repeating the words
all the way down. Bam! Slam 'em on paper.

My Job Here

Afternoons, I walk my usual local route:
Sixth Street to First, school to post office,
tidying up the whole town in one easy stroll,
from blue dumpster to blue dumpster,
doing my self-appointed job.

Pop cans and occasional Budweiser,
rusty screws or once an old horse shoe,
a school note dropped on the way home,
McDonald's trash from up in The Dalles,
or a coffee cup from We 3,

maybe a shiny scrap of a party balloon
but never a used condom or needle,
mostly candy wrappers, Jolly Ranchers,
sucked lollipop sticks out by the swings.
I suppose I should mention

the taped windows, trucks with dead tires,
TV flicker through bent blinds. But also
the young boys after school, how they stop
me and my dog in the street, tickled to find
an instant Granny who'll listen.

Fly-over Country at Night

Two stars between the clouds
or they might be planets,
a high jet on its way to the big city,

gleam of my dog's wet nose
sniffing frost-glitter in the grass,
the 9 pm silence of Court Street.

The dog and I circle the block.
In the worn parsonage next door,
a TV plays to a darkened room..

What
can Pastor Tony Baker be watching
more sacred than this cold night?

I want to knock on Tony's front door
to proselytize about miracles, but
I shove my fists into my pockets.

For Example

If for example I were to say lupine
and you didn't know lupine

and then I said blue
you wouldn't know which blue

and if I said deep blue almost purple,
you still wouldn't see it

which is why I want to grab your hand
and drag you up "D" Hill —

("D" for the white-painted stones
graduating seniors repaint each year)

where if you kneel between rabbit brush
and the miscellaneous grasses

and peer through the blooming lupine
you can open your arms to embrace

the long ridge of the horizon
and the whole little village down below

until the words *furtive* and *false-hearted*
drop out of your vocabulary

in this most absolutely perfect week
of a year of perfect weeks

here on the top of our hill
where Linda and Sandy leave a bowl

and a plastic gallon jug full of water
in case someone's dog might get thirsty

Sunrise with One Surviving Apple Tree

In scraggly woods
at the east edge of Mount Hood forest,

charred chimney bricks
and a few square-headed nails –

not the baby in his starched white skirts,
not the farmer's diligent wife

murmuring to her leghorn hens.
This fall, one final misshapen apple

pecked at by crows, and here
in leaf mold lit up by sunrise,

a silent scuffling
as of high-buttoned shoes.

If you bit into that last apple,
it would taste whiter than new snow

on the dawn-pink slope of Mount Hood.
It would taste like the song

your own great-grandmother
sang to her chickens

each morning to help them lay.
The song had no words.

The song had no words
and you, you can croon them all.

FALL

Home Game

I'm wearing no hat to take off,
don't put my hand over my heart,

as I step onto my front porch
and turn toward the football field.

Out there on the fifty-yard line
John Hickox squeezing the mike:

...at the twilight's last gleaming...
Alone on my porch I sing full voice.

Coin toss: We choose to receive.
Thanks, Dufur. I receive so much.

Manning Up

Between rows of pick-ups and cars
in the lighted high school parking lot
next to the perfectly chalked football field,
a skinny eight-year-old boy comes skipping

until he glances up at the bald coach
and the whole high school football team
armored in shoulder pads. Now the boy
switches to man-stride, solid, heavy, hulking,

deliberate, his hair still soft and mussed
like a puppy. I'm not this boy's mother
but somewhere inside me an iron portcullis
drops against soldiers massed at the castle wall.

Another Afternoon Practice

Hey, it's my turn to be last,
yells one boy in his red t-shirt.

He jogs behind the line of kids,
grinning.

I would appoint him
CEO of every global corporation

or maybe President.
No, really I want to marry him.

White-faced Calf

The calf lies alone with a rubber bucket of water
in this small temporary pen

He lies all alone here under November frost
and the wide band of the Milky Way

His face shines between metal bars
in the dark lot behind the school

His face shines where he lies on his own dung
under starlight as I walk with my dog before bed

My dog sticks her head through the metal bars
and sniffs at the border of manure

I reach through the metal bars
and pat the bony crest of his white head

I have visited him night after night
for over a month

I think I am writing a memoir about this calf
and small-town loneliness

Because You Never Had Your Fifth Birthday

– for Nettie B., Pioneer Cemetery
Nov 7 1893 - Oct 16 1898

The iron fence around your stone
is almost the size of a baby's crib.

Dear Nettie, today is your birthday.
Let me give you this old baby doll.

Her porcelain head has pursed lips
and real hair in marcelled waves.

Her hands have wrists that swivel
so she can help weed your grave.

Center Ridge School, Wasco County

Metal pipes for swings,
an unpainted outhouse
leaning into the wheat field.

Is it wind from the canyon
or shrill voices of children
shaking the loose boards?

On the whitewashed wall
a tall unbroken blackboard
erased for the last time.

No glass in the windows.
Instead of a school bell,
birds up in the tower.

Nests and white streaks
from decades of nestlings
fledged from this tower.

Fallen to the dirt cellar,
scraps of notebook paper
turned almost into earth.

Whose fingers perfected
Palmer method letters
on pages with printed lines?

Down beyond Kelly Cutoff
an old stove-up rancher
longs for the school marm.

After This Morning's Dogwalk

On this clear November morning,
the whole town seemed aglow
like our local snowy mountain
or my bouncy white dog.

Now the dog and I arrive home,
one of us repeating phrases.
The dog bends to her water bowl
while I hurry over to my desk.

You're always working on poems,
comments my sweet man,
but I can't quite agree. *No,* I say,
trying to explain my life to him,

it's those cockamamie poems —
how they're always working on me.

WINTER

All Is Calm, All is Bright

Our town has lit the big star on Dufur Hill,
its heavy orange extension cord draping
across snow crust.

Below, in lit houses, we all cook supper.
Good smells season our rooms. Even
the poorest neighbors will eat.

I hope they won't turn on their huge TV's
to hear about one family in a distant war
where rescue agencies can't go.

An unnamed family, their young children,
shiver together beside a makeshift stove
welded from galvanized scrap.

All the chairs gone. That family is burning
their leather shoes. The shoes of children
offer little heat.

Winter Song

Up here on our hill, the frost bells ring:
each wand of grass is sparkling.

Come climb the rutted gravel road
whose diamond pebbles glow.

Sing as you walk down Dufur Hill
where spangled tumbleweed rolls.

What blows beneath the cattle gate
will glitter on local streets

like snow-haired men in pick-ups slowing
to wave in the silver morning.

Snow Day

Snow fog holds surrounding hills
in its pale gold glow.

The infrequent crunch of tires
over hardened icy ridges.

The yellow herd of school buses
asleep under white blankets.

Tonight's Christmas concert
put off until tomorrow at 10 a.m.

In a red hat with tassel and bell,
a small girl jingles, slides, twirls.

Ah, *Joy to the World* or at least,
on this fine morning, Joy in Dufur.

Epiphany

Today, a good hour before sunset,
I tromped up our hill to see the star.

The star has a plain metal frame
strung with Christmas lights.

It stands on a flimsy scaffold, not far
off the ground. My dog came too,

sampling cow pies. All the puddles
were frozen over. Say, have the Kings

arrived at the stable? Any day now
the town will shut off its star, store it

behind the cinder block utility shed
where deer like to sleep. But I,

true nonbeliever, will go on believing
in the wondrous star of Dufur –

homemade star on conduit pipe,
oh, ye star of black electrical tape.

January

January come round again
and we're spreading on our toast
plum preserves put up by the dead

The Old Juniper Fencepost

The squared-off post with twists in the grain,
its wood grayed with years,
the post somebody's father's father
cut and shaped with an axe
and dug and pounded into place,
the post that once held five strands of barbed wire
along the southern end of the uphill wheat field,
the original post that stood up and kept serving
before it leaned so far over for so long,
it was replaced with a green metal fencepost,
that old juniper post spent four generations
being useful.

I could wish as much for myself.

This morning the fencepost lies resting
aslant on the ground, its whole decaying length
bejeweled with frost.

Plagiarized Tragic Poem

    – found inked on the riser of one of the wooden bridges
    to the park, two days before Valentine's Day

I wish he'd loved
because what I say is true
no matter what happens
I do love YOU
even if your to shy
I'll be here for you
because I'm just a ghoust to you

    manonymous

Valentine for My Husband

You are a constant riffle in Fifteen Mile Creek,
one raindrop on the tip of a thorn bush, glistening.

You are a rock outcropping where small creatures
hide from the farmer's circling combine.

Tonight you are the mountain's lenticular hat
and also the sunset staining that same hat crimson.

You are the great bell in front of the schoolhouse
summoning me daily to faithful attendance:

here from my wooden bench as I study kindness
let me offer you this polished apple. Call it a kiss.

The Days Start Getting Longer

Fog frosts my eyelashes
like spangles on fence posts.

Gods and beasts
sleep in the same landscape,

and although on some days
I can't distinguish

the one from the other,
I do understand

I'm too late to be a beast
and still too young to be a god

though I expect to get there
wearing my mother pelt.

Meanwhile,
under this high white meadow,

the roots of lupine
are dreaming of Spring–

my only blue-eyed child.

Full Moon

Our moon is as yellow as a town streetlight
hanging above the slope of the mountain.

Hush.

Walk with me out Dufur Valley Road
due west toward the old Ramsey Grange.

Look.

The glowing mountain keeps getting bigger.

Vocabulary Words for the SAT's

I won't say anything *derogatory* about the *maelstrom*
of 3x5 cards like *flotsam* along my side of Court Street,

about the *impropriety*, the *exigency* of cleaning up
this unwanted *largesse* of language in front of my house.

Some *feckless* high school student must have lost them
unless a *nefarious* bully tossed them from the school bus.

After my eyes conduct a *reconnaissance* of the *morass*,
my *insatiable* orderliness sets me *summarily* to work.

Some cards I *extricate* from dry weeds, others I *exhume*
from *brackish* puddles. I *glean* cards from the ditch.

Each card *delineates* meaning and usage, some words
outré, others *superannuated*, a true *gallimaufry**

for a *logophile.*

          * hodge-podge (not on the SAT's)

Bridge of the Gods

Each time I drive from Dufur to Portland or Portland
home to Dufur, I munch an apple in Cascades Locks
by exit 44 to the Bridge of the Gods which, despite
its romantic name, is just an old metal trestle bridge
over a narrowish place where Indians remember
and geologists confirm how an enormous rockslide
once spanned the wide Columbia.

I eat up my whole apple, entire core, seeds and all.
When nothing's left but the tiny woody stem, I toss
that stem onto the passenger seat rubber floor mat.
Apple stems collect like words scattered on a page,
like the too many prepositions I'm trying to discard,
or the word *still* which I tend to overuse in my quest
to connect future and past.

Now I'm tossing words onto lined paper as if words
will last long after the Bridge of the Gods collapses
into the river and what I am writing is unintelligible
to everyone except experts who also study Sanskrit,
but the word *apple* will have unaccountably endured,
and in an abandoned orchard one ancient apple tree
will re-seed itself, and come spring it might bloom.

SPRING

Wasco Woman

For a thousand generations
you have knelt on this stone
beside the snow-melt creek.

You were kneeling here before
the green-fringed Euphrates
reflected the towers of Babylon.

You knelt here long before
iron-rimmed wagon wheels
crushed spring onion grass.

You remember how to find
the gift of the camas root.
You are your own ancestor.

You have cupped your hands
to scoop cold water and dipped
your mouth to your hands.

Speak to me out of the water.
Please tell me the real name
for my Fifteen Mile Creek.

At last I am hearing her speak:
We called this stream Nansene.
I used to drink here with Coyote.

Ag Class in the School Parking Lot

Our March wind is still chilly
and the mountain bright white

beyond the end of the valley,
but wheat is greening on the hills.

This morning during second period
sixteen skinny tenth-graders —

no jackets, no hats — wait to drive
a small Kubota diesel front loader.

These are the kids, the grandkids,
neighbors of farmers and ranchers.

They practice doing turns and rows.
The machine gleams bright orange.

Too soon the buzzer for class-over
will buzz an end to this happy dance.

The teacher will turn off the engine
and watch the kids straggle inside,

their cheeks still shining. For once
they love each other and their town.

The class could be named *Civics*
or else *Phys Ed* or even *Geometry*,

but I propose we ought to call it *Art*.

I Don't Hear the Train

The Great Southern Railroad will no longer trace
the curving course

of Fifteen Mile Creek as it flows east and north
to the wide Columbia.

The train won't stop in Petersburg, in Fairbanks,
Brookhouse, Emerson, Wrentham —

towns that are mostly gone, names that persist
only on maps.

The daily train won't pull onto narrow hillside sidings
by grain elevators in Rice or Boyd.

No wood-sided hack sits ready to crank at the depot
just east of town

for transporting the traveling salesmen
to the three-story Balch hotel built of good local brick

where those salesmen spread catalogs and samples
in the maroon-draped parlor.

The train won't rattle south to the ghost town of Friend,
end of the line. Even the tracks are gone.

Only the songs of nighttime coyotes continue to travel
between the soft hills

where wheat in its regular parallel furrows still follows
the same irregular contours

wheat has followed for generations,
fields lying fallow every other year.

Between the high and reciprocal choruses of coyotes,
I lie awake listening

to the soft white wheat as it grows.

Our City Park on the Saturday before Easter Sunday

Bundled toddlers, close to the ground
over a lawn of scattered pastel eggs,
each tiny kid clutching a fancy bucket.

Pick them up, urges a bent grandfather,
Like this, say the mothers, leaning down.
The round toddlers squat in place, stuck

and confused, their chubby legs wide apart.
Pale sunlight tries to illuminate gray skies.
Nobody here in the park is ready to rise.

Interruption

1. The Journey

Whenever I have to fly east out of Portland, I always book seat 31 F which is far enough back that the right wing of the Boeing 737 won't block my view, and I sit at attention, cheek to the window, as we gain speed and the plane takes off, lifting over the Columbia out of thick ground fog, and in a mere four minutes Mount Hood rises white under its lenticular cloud almost next to my window, and I can see due south to Mount Jeff and the Sisters, can look down past thinning forest slopes and the start of Dufur valley, past the high dry wheat fields and the sage canyons of the Deschutes and John Day Rivers and the flat Umatilla, and then I am in exile and already counting how many nights of being a pleasant guest until I can fly back, this direction in chosen seat 31 A which will be on the Hood side, meanwhile waiting all across the country for the small shadow of our jet to cross the Snake from Idaho back into Oregon where, as we finally approach the plateaus of wheat, as we cross the Deschutes, I can almost reclaim the body of my landscape, knowing that soon I will re-inhabit the landscape of my body.

2. The Magic Trick

So it's United flight #1551 from Newark to Portland, Oregon, flying west at 25,000 feet, and we're heading in south of the Columbia, and I'm in the window seat on the left, 31 A. Just before we approach the Mount Hood forest I look down and spot the three grain elevators and the long roof of the Dufur school and, yes, that might even be my little house with its green metal roof just across the street from the school, and I say to myself, *Penelope, why are you sitting in this plane which will soon be landing at PDX when you'd much rather be right down there in Dufur?* So I dematerialize through the glass and reassemble myself and glide gently down over wheat fields, tilting my arms to steer. I don't care that I have abandoned my carry-on under the seat in row 31 because everything I need is already down in the little house with the green roof, and I think there's even a strawberry yogurt left in the icebox, and we all know that yogurt stays good long past its printed expiration date.

Birthday Poem in April

From across the street, piercing shouts
of school kids at recess

From my black locust tree, deep lament
of mourning doves

long white bridal bouquets of the locust
not yet in bloom

For seventy-some years I've been married
to this blue, blue sky

That middle school girl moping on a swing,
skirt tucked between her knees,

I want to run across Sixth Street and tell her
Look up past the crossbar

Honey, it gets better   Better and better

Remembering Ninth Grade

Ninth grade. Last period Social Studies.
I sucked hard on my bare upper arm.

Escape.

My skin tasted of May.

For the Schoolgirl Hunched under a Juniper Bush

So I ask myself, How's a girl supposed to voice
a would-be Advice Poem?

Well, not exactly a girl. A quote "older woman."
Let's try this version:

Like, hey, honeybunch, listen up.
Not my first rodeo. Been around that block.

I do know diddly-squat.
Hell, I've slept with diddly-squat.

Or stop right there. As my dad used to say,
Don't go being such a gosh darn fool

because, hey, sweetie pie, I really do,
in this one close moment between us,

I really do love you. You are the first crocus,
the froglet on the lily pad, my baby's toes,

and here's what I need to tell you:
It's none of it real and it won't last,

so wear your reddest lipstick and tip a bit
of Bombay gin into that tame vanilla milkshake.

And oh, lambykins, remember to be kind.

In My Home Village

All night coyotes crooned around my bed.
This morning four school girls in hoodies

came to write poems at my kitchen table
and I was happy like an oak with acorns.

When the local fire siren sounded at noon,
horses down by the creek lifted their heads.

The afternoon was perfect. Our wet planet
kept rotating without my close supervision

while the cold North Pole and South Pole
called to each other through molten rock.

As Dufur Hill rolled east to block the sun,
clouds above the mountain throbbed pink.

Just now a rainbow trout swam me to bed
where the Dipper drips sleep on my eyes.

I think dying might feel like this – luscious
and complete, the tremble after the love.

Memorial Day

The hill is blue lupine, and the meadowlark trills
from the highest point above our peaceful town.

On Main Street the Grand Marshall of the parade
rides by in a model-T sporting his WWII medals.

In the cemetery down the road, other soldiers
sleep under packed dirt. Nobody has told them

how all those young men are still out there dying,
how they keep dying and dying all over the world

in every month of the year. I think each blue hill
or valley or delta or prairie is home to someone.

Why can't they stay home being happy and well?

The Year They Drafted the Grandmothers

The process began with the government letter
excerpted at length in the following paragraphs:

Under Article 36, Section 24, Paragraph 37 of the Selective Service System, your number was submitted by your local board to fulfill this quarter's draft quota for two years military service.

You are hereby notified to appear at the Induction Center for processing into the United States Army. Meal vouchers will be furnished at the Center during the two day process. Following a physical and mental examination, aptitude tests, haircut, and government-issued clothing, you and other inductees will be transported for eight weeks of basic training.

Please get your personal affairs in order.

This letter was sent to selected grandmothers
seventy and older because it took that long

for said grandmothers to be fit to serve.
It took carrying and birthing and nursing and loving

a fragile new human until that human
survived the long vicissitudes

of growing up. It took more years
of carrying that hard knot in the gut

because it's your kid and you care too much.
Live through all that to become a soldier.

Now follow the Matriarch with her stars and bars.

She will not shoot. You will not shoot.

You will stroke the cheek of the enemy soldier,
that almost beardless cheek. You will say

Honey, go home. This isn't your fight.
Some rich old men are making you do this.

Go kiss your girl. She's waiting for you.
Go make a grandkid for your loving mother.

And the boys will go home alive and undamaged.
The girls and the mothers will hug them so hard

that the rich old men will have to give up.
Let this be the story the grandmothers tell.

Please Be So Kind as to Cut These Out and Distribute Them as Bookmarks

- -

War: a condition in which powerful elders on one or both sides command a group of young people to make holes in the living bodies of another group of young people in order to settle an argument between the elders.

- -

War: a condition in which powerful elders on one or both sides command a group of young people to make holes in the living bodies of another group of young people in order to settle an argument between the elders.

- -

War: a condition in which powerful elders on one or both sides command a group of young people to make holes in the living bodies of another group of young people in order to settle an argument between the elders.

- -

War: a condition in which powerful elders on one or both sides command a group of young people to make holes in the living bodies of another group of young people in order to settle an argument between the elders.

- -

War: a condition in which powerful elders on one or both sides command a group of young people to make holes in the living bodies of another group of young people in order to settle an argument between the elders.

- -

War: a condition in which powerful elders on one or both sides command a group of young people to make holes in the living bodies of another group of young people in order to settle an argument between the elders.

War: a condition in which powerful elders on one or both sides command a group of young people to make holes in the living bodies of another group of young people in order to settle an argument between the elders.

War: a condition in which powerful elders on one or both sides command a group of young people to make holes in the living bodies of another group of young people in order to settle an argument between the elders.

War: a condition in which powerful elders on one or both sides command a group of young people to make holes in the living bodies of another group of young people in order to settle an argument between the elders.

War: a condition in which powerful elders on one or both sides command a group of young people to make holes in the living bodies of another group of young people in order to settle an argument between the elders.

Knowledge of Good and Evil

I am a way better biter than Eve
or Adam. I go at apples entirely,
core and seeds, leaving nothing
but stem. I have built my house
out of stems, and between them,
a window. All these ageing years
l have stared out. Eve swallowed
while Adam watched and then bit.
You know the bitter punishment:
I groaned twice during childbirth,
uttered *Excuse me.* I am a cloud
above my two cottonwood trees,
in greenest love with their heart-
shaped leaves. My sweet babies
grow up and leave, though they
lurk under old bark. A skinny kid
yells *Dude* across the ballfield.
He can't imagine when his feet
in sneakers grew so enormous,
able to smash a fallen apple flat.
Far away in the city, a streetcar
clangs on its tracks like money,
throwing sparks. Before I travel
further into the dark, I'll swallow
the worm in the apple and let it
replace my human voice. Bless
all the worms who comprehend
how stories can end in violence.
Or is *struggle* life's given name?
I admired this planet most when
marmosets were the grown-ups
and no human – *sapiens* or less
sapient – yet prowled this earth,
before any man hoisted a spear.

Do Not Despair

A veiled woman stands tall
under stars. Every night
she rotates the shining sky.
She sprinkles stars like sugar.
Some of her stars are old,
others are not yet visible.
She's been busy tending to stars
since before the beginning of counting.

On earth she has four children
and each child is beloved:
water for spilling through channels,
air for accommodating shapes,
dirt for its sandy grit,
and fire for lighting the sky.
The woman guards all night.
Her name is *Do not despair*.

In her netted veil she watches
as a mama skunk drinks
from a stream that ripples
over rocks.
Four tiny kits
sleep in a hidden burrow
under the luster of stars.
The skunk's white stripe
might be the Milky Way.

SUMMER
(and FIRE SEASON)

Lesson of the Ordinary

This morning I carried the morning sun lightly
over my right shoulder.

The knots on the top wire strung between posts
made barbed stars against blue sky.

I saw two butterflies, one bright yellow, the other
black against the graveled track.

But the two butterflies were really just one butterfly
casting a black butterfly shadow.

Now I suspect the yellow butterfly is the real world
where I am the shadow.

In the Season of the Burn Ban

June too hot, early green
baked from the hillsides,
lupines flowered and done
or dried into purple straw,
our exposed summer legs
stabbed with cheatgrass,
even the pointed mountain
shedding snow too soon.
At the Ranger Station a sign
raised by Smokey the Bear:
FIRE DANGER HIGH.
     And yet,
with our fine new fire station,
our faithful fleet of fire engines,
our quorum of good old boys
who carry dedicated pagers
on the dashboards of pick-ups
or in worn pockets of overalls,
who carry big tanks of water
in the backs of their trucks,
with local dogs ready to howl,
we are safe. We are so safe.

Listening to the Morning

You can hear it all too:
the flat triangle of mountain against sky,
intense blue down to the round horizon,
golden wheat fattening its sweet kernels,
the lightest wind playing the barbed wire,
bent grids of outdated antennae,
a rusty satellite dish lifting its torn mesh.

A single hawk cruises for slow mice,
one local lizard suns on a warm stone,
a dragonfly like a double-winged bi-plane
but wide as a hummingbird comes dipping
where late lupine tilts toward July sun,
and salsify lifts its oversized dandelion fuzz.
Last week's shocking mariposa lily is gone.

Maybe those hot magenta petals of the lily
were just too noisy for this quiet morning
where a white dog pants ever so softly
in the sparse shade of dried bunch-grass
while a sun-baked woman with wild hair
perches a long time on her favorite rock,
listening.

Celebration

On a day that will top 100 degrees
everyone in town wakes up early.

An orchard guy is flat-topping bushes
in the Underhills' perfect yard.

When I head up the hill at 6:30 a.m.
Jay is out washing one of his Chevrolets.

Soon the old ranchers at Kramer's Market
will be gathering for coffee.

Blessèd be the great *-ings* of the world,
gather-ings, gleam-ing like the metal pole

right up through the center of a globe,
the pole that holds our little earth turn-ing.

When I sat in a classroom spin-ning the globe,
I hadn't known I was pray-ing.

Cub Scout Car Wash in the School Parking Lot

(July 21, after the Substation Fire had jumped the Deschutes River to burn in
the next county)

Out by the curb four boys
in matching red t-shirts
jump up and down

with hand-printed signs:
Car wash! Car wash!
They like jumping.

Now a kid by the fence,
starts spraying before
I close my window.

Two fathers wash roofs,
a sister brushes tires,
a mother watches.

A boy clutching a puppy
wanders in puddles.
My car stays dirty

but now it's dirty and wet.
Pay whatever you want.
I hand over ten bucks.

A fine Saturday afternoon.
Blacktop glitters in sun.
Everyone is happy.

No hungry refugees here.
No wars. The great fire
far across the river.

Old Survivor

– Long Hollow Fire near Dufur, Oregon, July 2018

Acres of ripe unharvested wheat burned.
Dry roadside turned black.

But old Center Ridge School didn't burn down.
Beams and bell tower didn't smolder.

The front porch and two cloakrooms
didn't catch on fire.

The warped floor where children stomped
didn't collapse.

The cracked back wall with the blackboard
didn't burn down.

The vanished textbooks and writing tablets
didn't burn up.

The missing windowpanes didn't crack.
No smoke rushed up the rusted stove pipe.

No teacher ushered the children
out past the swings and outhouses.

All the old students are safe as ghosts.
They can recite their multiplication tables.

They can name all the state capitals.
They know where they are buried.

Dance of the Fire Imps

One tiny fire imp leapt out
from under Bucky's enormous combine.

A single spark struck a ripe head of wheat.
It charred the beard around the kernels.

The spark skittered down the hollow stalk,
laughing.

The fire imp summoned all his friends.
They hid under stubble until they flared

in a red line between furrows.
They somersaulted to the edge of the field.

By the time Bucky noticed, it was too late.
By then the imps were playing with the wind.

They raced the length of Easton canyon
and scrambled up over Tygh Ridge.

They skimmed down through more wheat
until they reached the cool Deschutes river.

A fire imp can't swim but watch how he flies.
Thirty-seven thousand burnt acres later

over parts of two counties, the fire imps
are still dancing.

From three canyons over, their music rises
orange and black in the sky.

Worst Fire Season on Record

All day the doves
hid among leaves,
jaunty quail
failed to parade.
Even the finches
ditched the feeder.
Not a sparrow
pecked at the ground.

The valley stayed narrow
and smoke-yellow.
All the mountains
didn't exist.
Everyone in town
ate smoke for supper.
The quarter moon
shown dim orange.

Even the dog
sagged on the couch,
her hipbones
defeated.
Don't tell me
this is the hottest year on record.
I already know
this is the driest year on record.

I hesitate to think
how this world will end:
the small lizards
crouched among rocks,
their whole elastic bodies
breathing out, breathing in.

Walking My Dog Late at Night While Several Hundred Firefighters Are Asleep at the School across the Street, I Meet a Young Man Standing Alone by the Dumpster

Hi, there (I say to him in the yellow circle of the street light)

    Hi.

So are you one of the firefighters?

    Yup.

Well, thank you so much for being here.

    Glad to help out.

If you don't mind my asking, what made you decide to be a firefighter?

    (Here the young man leans down and pets my dog)

    My mom wouldn't let me join the Marines.

Fire Report

– August 3, 2018

In the kitchen of the school cafeteria
Becky and I stood at a makeshift counter
slicing 140 heads of romaine lettuce
to make salad for the 400 fire fighters
headquartered in the school parking lot

Terry was opening enormous cans
to make spaghetti sauce for 400 people
I have no idea how many cans it took
None of us wore those little hairnets
like the lunch ladies in old cafeterias

A red-faced young man replaced bags
in the gray industrial garbage pails
The district superintendent stopped by
to see whether we needed anything
He's also the high school football coach

Someone reported the wind had shifted
and we wondered aloud whose farm
between which of the back roads
Becky and I kept slicing up lettuce
We were getting really fast at our job

A farmer just a few miles south of us
ignited his best crop of wheat in years
to create a fire break that might save
his neighbor's house and outbuildings
Somebody's horses panicked and ran

This morning my house smells smoky

and I can see smoke rising over the hill
The missing horses are still missing
The wind is blowing seriously now
I have no good ending for this report

1 Killed in the 80,000-acre Fire near The Dalles

— compiled from local news reports

1

One person has died
Wasco County Sheriff's office
Man's body found
Creating a fire line
Protect his neighbor's property
Near a burned out tractor
Clearing a strip of land
Wasco County authorities
Identified as John Ruby*
Overcome by fire
The kind of neighbor who

2

This sad morning
in the Dufur school gym
on folding chairs and bleachers
we listened to stories
about Big John
and dabbed at our eyes.
John always pointed with two fingers.
He square-danced on horseback.
After the service
there was plenty of food.
The cafeteria's baked beans
were especially tasty.

* A burnt kitten rescued from the fire was given to
John Ruby's widow who named him Little John

After the Fires in Wasco County, Oregon

In the midst of his 3,000 acres of ruined wheat
he stands with a pad and pencil.

The red-tailed hawks who swooped for rodents
have all departed the county.

The dog who has followed him out to the fields
frantically licks at her paws.

He has just 72 hours to file his claim for crop loss
while the black dirt still smolders.

This was promising to be a great year for wheat.
Now he tallies defeat by the bushel.

A Story about Fire

I don't know why the Oregon Department of Forestry decided to drive one of its vans up Dufur Hill, the hot underside of the vehicle brushing tall, dry weeds on a day when multiple thousands of acres of grass and wheat are already on fire. *Park in a clear spot*, I shout. The driver asks, *Are you the landowner?* No, I say, *this is Stan's land*. But I could claim it as my land too and also it's my rock where several mornings each week in every season I sit looking across at two mountains and on the clearest days four mountains. Today there are no mountains.

I don't know how the burnt stumps on Susan and Duane's fire-scoured land managed to turn into vertical pits of ash. Their in-laws Becky and Steve are over there putting out hot spots.

I don't know who decided to haul away the rows of blue port-a-potties from the fire headquarters in the school parking lot before the Long Hollow fire was completely extinguished. A day later the port-a-potties are back for the spreading South Valley fire. But the mobile kitchens aren't back. We locals are making supper for 400 fire fighters. My job is cutting up lettuce. Lots of romaine lettuce.

I do know why John Ruby died next to his burnt tractor. He was discing a fire line trying to save somebody's house.

Today the newest fire is 60% contained. The temperature will be over 100 degrees and in the afternoon the wind will rise. Maybe I'm telling you a story about love.

What I Told My Dog This Morning

Hey, it's harder to tie my shoes
while you're licking my nose.

I love you too. Let's go now
before the day gets too hot.

Okay, come on through the gate
so I can re-hitch the chain.

Why must you do it on the path
just when I didn't bring a bag?

Cow chips don't work well
for shoveling up fresh dog shit

but this small rock will serve
only because I have hands.

And sometimes I have to wonder
just who threw the first rock

at another creature with hands?
Killing ought to be done with teeth

like you, dog, as you shake that vole.
Now I'm thinking of old Everett

fighting island to island in the Pacific,
of all the boys who went to war

seventy-some years back. Their wrists
so thin, hands trembling, or bones.

First Dinner-Plate Sunflower

I know what heaven looks like.
My white dog lies like a lamb, head up,

on the lawn which is graced with dandelions
and white morning glories.

The hawk who intended to catch a mouse
soars higher into the sky.

The first huge sunflower of the season unfurls
like separating day from darkness.

There is no blue
like August right above Dufur.

The arched back-and-forth sprinkler
spits dark spots onto freshly split kindling.

The red butt of the axe next to the woodpile
might be God's lost bandanna.

A Thought

We all know who's a cheapskate
and who used to hotwire cars.

Everybody is related to somebody
and we knew their grandparents,

or their kid is on the football team
or in Future Farmers of America.

If this world were more like Dufur,
could we stop killing each other?

Bumper Sticker

On an old pick-up truck parked by the hardware store:

I've been fishing so long
my worm gets social security

The Only Blot on Our Storybook Perfection

You know the red house on NE 4th?
Where the shingles need painting?

You know.
Up past where Dena used to live.

Well, the husband shot the wife.

She lay all night on the floor.
He wouldn't let the kids touch her.

Then he drove away.
The cops nabbed him in Tygh Valley.

But those people weren't *from* here.

Creek in the Town of the Murder

Nobody in town yaks more than the creek.
It talks all night, speaking over stones.

What a long way it has come down the mountain.
It remembers the glacier but can't go back.

Blood flowing into her body, rifle holes closing,
their marriage quarrel unclenching.

So late at night, and who outside on the street
listening? Not the blathering creek.

Our Own Little Chapter from the Tale of the Oregon Trail

This local creek knows only its own small story:
how here between treeless hills, covered wagons

forded the stream, wagons that chose the inland route,
because of too many drownings in the Columbia,

too many wagons lined up for rafts, no forage left,
hundreds of draft animals near to starving. Even today

this creek still speaks of those yoked oxen, their huge
leathery tongues. If I think I taste them in the water,

I'm probably wrong.

106 Degrees

All afternoon the sun hangs out overhead,
laying its heat down every street

I try to walk under the shade of branches
but the shade is so narrow

I might as well try to stay cool in the shade
of a local utility pole

or in the thinner shade
of its two wires

On Top of the Hill Again

From here I can see a full circle of horizon
Snow is getting patchy on the mountains
Three of my five best high school friends are dead
My young dog has bounded uphill on springy legs
She is not my first and will not be my last dog
My husband has stayed home with his usual aches
He is not my first but will be my last husband
The wheat is harvested and the grain elevators are full
Yellow stubble embraces the contours of the hills

Last night the Perseid meteors flashed over my backyard
Today is our annual harvest festival
Pampered horses and John Deeres will parade
The queen of the Wasco County Fair will wave like a queen
The firemen will toss Tootsie Rolls to the sidewalk crowd
I will slip one into my pocket and forget to eat it
Later I'll browse at garage sales all over town
I'll poke through neighbors' boxes of loose miscellany
But what more on this earth could I possibly need?

Harvest

Here in the cemetery I position a stone puppy on my future grave.
To my right, old Everett and Betty lie buried knowing I'll join them.
To my left, Becky and Steve will likely arrive some years after me.
Meanwhile, this puppy will mouth and mouth her little stone shoe
and never dent it.

Beyond the fence, a red Case International combine model 2388
mows its wide swath. The arm pumps grain into the waiting truck.
I am watching the living heart of wheat country, its golden blood,
but I can no longer write the word *heart* in a poem since my son
survived two open heart surgeries.

Now a heart has become a heart, never a metaphor. His heart
is repaired and beats with an audible click. Now the white truck
is full up and off to the grain elevator. A line of trucks unloading.
Lines of stubble. Lines in a poem. Lifelines. Only this stone dog
will go on, and not forever.

The heated earth, the asteroid, rubble of all our human forgetting,
and the little stone puppy like a god presiding over all our bones,
what does it come to? Delight, delight, delight for each moment
we notice and label. To walk a row of wheat the combine missed
and bite into one ripe kernel.

Everett's Dodge

I am inventing a biography for this old Dodge pick-up. It's permanently parked near the dead end on 6th and has wood blocks under the front wheels. The rust isn't rust-colored so much as green and pink and gold. A neighbor told me it used to belong to Everett Marvel. The last license plate is 1955, but the truck seems much older than that. I looked up various models of Dodge trucks, and this one is pretty old so Everett must have bought it used. When he came home with a medal for bravery and what we now call PTSD – he had enlisted as a Marine and was part of the bloody fighting to re-take one Pacific island after another – he wouldn't have had the cash to buy a new truck. He was too messed up and angry to hold a real job where he had to work for someone else. Instead he helped farm his father's land. Cattle and wheat. The farm is out in the canyon near where the old Shellrock schoolhouse used to be. Everett was already in his 90's when he drove me over there in a new white Honda. Nothing is left of the school but a foundation and the water pump out in front. The farm still has a small house and a big barn. I don't know how many years Everett drove this truck. I don't know how long ago he sold it or who drove it next or after that. There's no hay left in the bed. Nothing but country air. Everett is gone. Now I want to step up and slide onto the passenger side of the torn bench seat and reach across the big gear shift and pat the indent where he sat. I want to walk down 6th Street in the dark and climb into the rusted bed of the truck and lie down on my back to look for Everett among the clear stars.

HOME GALAXY

Piling Stones

The Great Chain of Being
ranks nine orders of angels
rates mammals above reptiles
down to the humblest pebble

I am building a pile of stones
I am loving this pile of stones
Today one small baby lizard
scoots from between stones

I am building without a plan
not constructing some temple
I'm worshiping no gods here
not really intending a cairn

so I don't arrange my stones
I plop 'em on top of the heap
If it's good enough for a lizard
hey, it's good enough for me

Apocrypha from unknown scroll hidden in a cave:

But the high places were not taken away —
the people piled stones in the high places.

Why I Heap Stones

If I keep walking this same hill
year after year after year, maybe

I will pile my stones high enough
to be visible from down below.

Meanwhile if anyone asks why
I am hauling all these stones,

here's my most honest answer:
No reason. Just for pure delight.

And believe me, some are heavy.
Those I carry a few feet at a time.

When I finally get them up there,
I am absurdly happy. This is not

important. Just a report.

Fog Cannot Illuminate the Past

From up here on this foggy hilltop,
no white mountain on the horizon,
no trio of tall silver grain elevators,
no houses, no creek down below.

Gone as those who died too young:
She was beautiful as the morning,
said my old grandfather just before
doctors cut out his fogged voice box.

If elk browse the high meadows
today they are invisible and yet
they belong to the same herd
from before the town was platted.

Long before pioneer wagon trains,
back even before the long before,
the first women in rush sandals
dug onions by Fifteen Mile Creek.

Nansene they called it back then.
Maybe the creek still remembers
but the water will no longer tell us
what its old name used to mean.

I Watch Myself Descending the Hill

The winding road is gravel, some places
dangerously loose.

When the poem-in-progress gets kicking
around in her mind,

she steps downhill with that flat duck-walk
her body recollects

from the heavy last month of pregnancy
half a century back.

News Hour

Wind combing dry yellow flowers of the rabbit brush.

The puppy's tag clinking as she dashes up slope.

Sneakers knocking loose gravel down the path.

A large flying insect click-clicking behind me.

Why should I listen to the politicians?

Night Feeding

The orphan calf emptied two large bottles
and then she suckled hard on my thumb.

Under stars, the high red blink of a plane.
My middle-aged kids so many states away,

and that old tightness filling my breasts.

Bless the Old Wheat Farmers

Bless their bellies and suspenders,
the tufts of white hair in their big ears,
their kindness, in spite of certain old
and politically incorrect ideas.

Let them hold open the post office door,
let them make the vestigial gesture
of half way reaching up to touch
stained bills of John Deere caps.

Let them sit together at the coffee joint,
broad shoulders not quite touching,
let them talk wheat prices or which girl
here in town had to get married,

and let them feel studly and also tender.
Who doesn't like thinking about sex,
no matter if it's been a long time?
They swallow their cooled-off coffee.

They have pushed the rock of their years
up the sloped wheat fields for a lifetime,
and that big old rock gets smoother now
even as strength goes out of their arms.

Let the rock roll down gently at the end,
not wrecking the expensive new combine.
Let the living old guys wear clean shirts
to the funerals and study their fingernails

as they dream about seeding or harvest.

His Boots

Everett's hard-used work boots
still stand side by side
tucked behind his TV tray
next to his big leather chair.

The boots face into the room
where Betty sits on the couch,
dinner plate on her TV tray.
She isn't eating.

She slides the tines of her fork
under the pork and beans,
then lays the fork handle
over the rim of her plate.

*My daughter took his sock*s
and put them in the wash.
Frayed tips of the laces
drape onto the rug.

Don't you see him? asks Betty.
I can see him
standing there in his boots.
Dirt on his boots like the grave.

The Illusive Farmhouse across the Valley

There may be a farmhouse
with its sway-back barn

I lived there in a dream
where I loved the farmer

His hips were knobs
under smudged coveralls

My hips were hungry
in the John Deere's shadow

He was a very old man
or maybe we never met

Country Mailbox in High Weeds

Its door gapes open, the metal flag
still up and rusted in place.

Nothing to send, nothing to deliver
but time. The final resident resides

under dirt.
I scribble a neighborly note:

> *Don't worry. The sky is watching*
> *over your old abandoned house*

Finding the Correct Viewpoint

Dry weeds catch in your bumper.
There's a high rock in the way.
You get out and shove it over.

The track keeps getting rougher
but you've always wanted to find
a viewpoint above the Deschutes.

The next rock is too big to move
and it might scrape your oil pan.
You abandon your car and keys

to go tromping through sage brush.
You open and latch the cattle gate
with your best country manners.

You follow the path around a cliff
until you can peer into the canyon
where water whitens over rapids.

You kick at your mother's words
you've been tripping over too long.
They fall so far you hear nothing.

You rename them *mercy beads*.
All these years you have wanted
to stand exactly here.

Woman Remembering Her Mother

When you were small, your mother
gazed at you with inexplicable grief.

She wanted to say, *For my whole life
I have hoped to be known.* But you

were a child so you couldn't see her.
Such a long darkness between you –

I can't explain why I weep now.

Now

At last

I can wait on both sides of the same door

holding yesterday and tomorrow

in my gentled hands.

Leaf on the Hill

There are no trees on the hill
have never been any trees on this hill

just wheat furrows and a gravel road
a telephone tower and some TV dishes

warped fence posts and barbed wire
squared stones edging an old pit

The leaf is tan-brown with speckles
and an invisible undercast of green

The veins on the leaf don't line up
its edges not serrated but scalloped

The leaf is dry and smells of nothing
If the woman believed that souls exist

this is exactly how her soul would look

Coyote's Babies Are Older than Their Mother

They have white in their whiskers.
They carry clouds in their heads.

They hold long songs in their eyes.
They sing all night from Dufur Hill.

Coyote's babies laugh under stars
but never let you in on the joke.

Meanwhile inside the sill of a cave
their mother twitches her gray ears.

She's taught her pups all she knows;
nothing she need do now but sleep.

Tonight

The red flash of an airplane
brushes another a star

while the creek
washes the flickery fish.

Meanwhile our home galaxy
spins in its spiral.

The dog shoves at my arm
with her insistent muzzle.

She whines *Rub my ears*.
Often,

at stray hours of the night,
I wonder whose pet I am.

Sunday Morning

The congregation sits in orderly pews
I sit on my usual rock

Becky plays the organ
My dog plays with tumbleweed

The congregation listens to Pastor Fain
I attend to the wind

Pastor Fain talks about loving Jesus
The wind sings about mountains

In church they lower their heads to pray
I raise my face to high blue sky

My dog licks my knee
We all understand we are blessed

Butterfly

A freckled white butterfly
flew before me
over the graveled track.

As it veered into the field
it touched down on
lupine and yellow salsify.

But I knew it wasn't an *it*.
That busy butterfly
had a gender and a plan

as authentic as my own. It
would do stuff,
butterfly stuff, until it died.

And after that, what? A thin
velvet smush.

Tonight the Sky is a Clear Pyrex Bowl Inverted over Our Little Town

You can see right through it
to stars on the inside and outside of the bowl.

A few come loose.
They sparkle as they fall into my waiting palms.

Each star is small and hard
and a lot cooler than you might have suspected.

I walk our tidy grid of streets
knocking at every house with its big TV still on.

Here, have some splendor, I say,
holding out the stars still cupped in my hands.

Such fine neighbors –
no one in town acts the slightest bit surprised.

Penelope Scambly Schott is a past recipient of the Oregon Book Award for Poetry. She lives a double life – in Portland where she and her husband host the White Dog Poetry Salon and in Dufur where she spends half of every week and also teaches an annual poetry workshop. Penelope climbs Dufur Hill regularly, always carrying the biggest stones she can lift to add to her rock pile.

Penelope Scambly Schott
604 NE Court Street
P.O. Box 536
Dufur, OR 97021